RAMKRISHNA

Gajanan Khergamker

JAICO PUBLISHING HOUSE

Ahmedabad Bangalore Bhopal Bhubaneswar Chennai
Delhi Hyderabad Kolkata Lucknow Mumbai

Published by Jaico Publishing House
A-2 Jash Chambers, 7-A Sir Phirozshah Mehta Road
Fort, Mumbai - 400 001
jaicopub@jaicobooks.com
www.jaicobooks.com

RAMKRISHNA
ISBN 81-7992-172-7

First Jaico Impression: 2003
Third Jaico Impression: 2008

Printed by
Repro India Limited
Plot No. 50/2, T.T.C. MIDC Industrial Area
Mahape, Navi Mumbai - 400 710

INTRODUCTION

Born in 1836 at Kamarpukur in West Bengal, Gadadhar Chatterjee was never formally educated but could read and write Bengali reasonably well. Though he was the son of a village priest, he was unable to read or speak Sanskrit and English.

For Gadadhar, popularly known later as Ramakrishna Paramhansa, his upbringing in an environment infused with devotion to Goddess Kali fetched him his first mystical trance at the age of seven. It led to a series of mystical occurrences later in which he claimed to have seen God as the Divine Mother, as Goddess Sita, as Rama, Krishna, Muhammad and Jesus Christ.

Sri Ramakrishna went on to become one of the most important nineteenth century Hindu mystics. His influence on his disciples, particularly Swami Vivekananda, led to the formation of an entire movement called the Ramakrishna Mission.

On God

Ramkrishna

It is God Himself who has become a physician. Therefore one must believe all of them. But one cannot have faith in them if one thinks of them as mere men.

There is only one who you may call your own and that is God.

God is engaged in three kinds of activity: creation, preservation and destruction.

Jiva is Shiva (all living beings are God). Who then dare talk of showing mercy to them ? Not mercy, but service, service. For man must be regarded as God.

Ramkrishna

He who is called Brahman by the gyanis is known as Atman by the yogis and as Bhagwan by the bhaktas.

The Lord has done so many things so will He not show people the way to worship Him? … He is our Inner Guide.

What need have I to know of his infinite splendours? If I must know these let me first realise him.

I accept God with form when I am in the company of people who believe in that ideal, and I also agree with those who believe in the formless God.

Ramkrishna

God can be seen. One can talk to Him as I am talking to you.

Is it possible to understand God's action and His motive? He creates, He preserves, and He destroys. Can we ever understand why He destroys?

In the Vedas creation is likened to the spider's web. The spider brings the web out of itself and then remains in it. God is the container of the universe and also what is contained in it.

Ramkrishna

Why run away from a tiger, which is also a manifestation of God?
The answer is: Those who tell you to run away are also manifestations of God; why shouldn't you listen to them?

On Salvation

Ramkrishna

No salvation is possible for man as long as he has desire, as long as he hankers for worldly things.

Friend, the more I live the more I learn.

There are six alligators — lust, anger, avarice and so on — within you, in the "soul's fathomless depths". But protect yourself with the turmeric of discrimination and renunciation and they won't touch you.

Ramkrishna

One cannot bring the holy image into a temple if the droppings of bats are all around. The eleven bats are our eleven organs, five of action, five of perception and the mind.

On Seeking God

Ramkrishna

Cry to the Lord with an intensely yearning heart and you will certainly see Him. People shed a whole jug of tears for wife and children. They swim in tears for money. But who weeps for God?

You see many stars in the sky at night, but not when the sun rises. Can you therefore say that there are no stars in the heavens during the day? O man, because you cannot find God in the days of your ignorance, say not there is no God.

Ramkrishna

Visit not miracle-mongers and those who exhibit occult powers. These men are stragglers from the path of Truth.

He is born in vain, who having attained the human birth, so difficult to get, does not attempt to realize God in this very life.

What is the use of making pilgrimages if you can attain the love of God remaining where you are?

Don't find fault with anyone, not even with an insect. As you pray to God for devotion, so also pray that you may not find fault with anyone.

Ramkrishna

Purify the spectacles of your mind and you will see that the world is God.

One should feel a yearning for God like the yearning of a person who has lost his or her job and is wandering from one office to another in search of work.

Seekest thou God? Then seek Him in man! His Divinity is manifest more in man than in any other object. Man is the greatest manifestation of God.

Whoever wants God intensely, finds Him. Go and verify it in your own life.

Ramkrishna

Living in solitude now and then, repeating God's name and singing His glories and discriminating between the real and the unreal these are the means to employ to see him.

On Love

Ramkrishna

First secure the oil of divine love, and then set your hand to the duties of the world.

Unalloyed love of God is the essential thing. All else is unreal. When one has love for God, one doesn't feel any physical attraction to wife, children, relatives and friends.

Do you know how a lover of God feels? His attitude is: 'Thou art my Father and Mother. Thou art the Whole, and I am a part.' He doesn't like to say, 'I am Brahman.'

Ramkrishna

If you enter the world without first cultivating love for God... You will be overwhelmed with its danger, its grief and its sorrows.

Lovers of God do not belong to any caste. The mind, body, and soul of a man are purified through divine love.

On Truth

Ramkrishna

I tell you the truth : there is nothing wrong in your being in the world. But you must direct your mind towards God.

Truth is one; only It is called by different names. All people are seeking the same Truth; the variance is due to climate, temperament and name.

Be not a traitor in your thoughts. Be sincere. Act according to your thoughts and you shall surely succeed. Pray with a sincere and simple heart, and your prayers will be heard.

Ramkrishna

It is said that truthfulness alone constitutes the spiritual discipline of the Kaliyuga (i.e. modern age). If a man clings tenaciously to truth he ultimately realizes God.

The world is indeed a mixture of truth and make-believe. Discard the make-believe and take the truth.

On Religion

Ramkrishna

All religions are true. God can be reached by different religions. Many rivers flow by many ways but they fall into the sea. They all are one.

A truly religious man should think that other religions also are paths leading to truth. We should always maintain an attitude of respect towards other religions.

Every man should follow his own religion. A Christian should follow Christianity, and a Mohammedan Mohammedanism. For the Hindu, the ancient path, the path of the Aryan rishis, is the best.

You must try all beliefs and traverse all the different ways once.

Ramkrishna

I have practiced all religions and I have also followed the paths of the different Hindu sects. I have found that it is the same God towards whom all direct their steps, though along different paths.

Let each man follow his own path (religion). If he sincerely and ardently wishes to know God... He will surely realize Him.

Dispute not. As you rest firmly in your own faith and opinion, allow others also equal liberty to stand by their own faith and opinion.

Ramkrishna

There is only one way to remove caste distinctions and that is by love of God. Through this divine love the untouchable becomes pure, the pariah no longer remains a pariah.

Every religion has errors. Everyone thinks that his watch alone gives the correct time. It is enough to have yearning for God.

On Women

Ramkrishna

Women whether naturally good or not, whether chaste or unchaste, should always be regarded as images of the Blissful Divine Mother.

If a man has sincere love for God, then all come under his control — the king, wicked persons and his wife.

On Wealth

Ramkrishna

Money can fetch you bread alone. Do not consider it as your sole end and aim.

He is truly a man to whom money is only a servant; but, on the other hand, those who do not know how to make a proper use of it, hardly deserve to be called men.

Those who cannot give up attachment to worldly things, and who find no means to shake off the feeling of 'I', should rather cherish the idea, 'I am God's servant; I am His devotee.'

Ramkrishna

The mind cannot dwell in God if it is immersed day and night in worldliness… it is necessary to go into solitude now and then and think of God.

Yes, there is no hope for a worldly man if he is not sincerely devoted to God.

On Modesty

Ramkrishna

Rain water never stands on high ground, but runs down to the lowest level. So also the mercy of God remains in the hearts of the lowly, but drains off from those of the vain and the proud.

The ego that asserts, 'I am the servant of God' is the characteristic of the true devotee. It is the ego of Vidya (Knowledge), and is called the 'ripe' ego.

To become great one must be humble. The tree laden with fruit always bends low.

Ramkrishna

As the dawn heralds the rising sun, so sincerity, unselfishness, purity, and righteousness precede the advent of the Lord.

Look at the anvil of a blacksmith — how it is hammered and beaten; yet it moves not from its place. Let men learn patience and endurance from it.

On Maya

Ramkrishna

Maya is nothing but 'woman and gold'. A man living in its midst gradually loses his spiritual alertness.

The mind and intellect become pure the moment they are free from attachment...

Remember that Maya keeps us in ignorance and entangles us in the world, whereas Daya makes our hearts pure and gradually unties our bonds.

Ramkrishna

Bondage is of the mind and freedom is also of the mind.

God alone, the Creator of this world-bewitching Maya, can save men from Maya. There is no other refuge but that great teacher.

On Bhakti

Ramkrishna

Bhakti is the one essential thing. To be sure that God exists in all beings.

Who, then is a devotee? He whose mind dwells on God. But this is not possible as long as one has egotism and vanity.

Wherein is the strength of a devotee? He is a child of God, and his devotional tears are his mightiest weapons.

You may desire Bhakti and pray for it. Practise the tamas of bhakti and force your demand upon the Divine Mother.

Ramkrishna

The heart of the devotee is the abode of God. He dwells, no doubt, in all things, but He especially manifests Himself in the heart of the devotee.

Bhakti, love of God, is the essence of all spiritual discipline. Through love one acquires renunciation and discrimination naturally.

One need not fear anything if one has received God's grace.

...Nor need a man have any fear whatever of the world if he attains sincere devotion by practicing spiritual discipline now and then in solitude.

Ramkrishna

In meditation one must be absorbed in God. By merely floating on the surface can you reach the gems lying at the bottom of the sea?

A devotee who possesses sattvic bhakti, meditates on God in absolute secret, perhaps inside his mosquito net while others think he is asleep.

O Mind, Forget the body, forget the sickness, and remain merged in Bliss!

Ramkrishna

Raga-bhakti is pure love of God, a love that seeks God alone and not any worldly end.

It (Raga-Bhakti) is like the cow's fondness for fodder mixed with oil-cake. The cow gobbles it down greedily.

On Selfless Work

Ramkrishna

Let me be condemned to be born over and over again, even in the form of a dog, if I can be of help to a single soul.

I will give up twenty thousand such bodies to help one man. It is glorious to help even one man.

The world is the field of action. Through action one acquires knowledge.

Through selfless work, the love of God grows in the heart. Then, through His grace, one realizes Him in course of time.

Ramkrishna

The guru instructs the disciple to perform certain works and refrain from others. He advises the pupil to perform action without desiring the result.

Even to chant the name and glories of God is work… Breathing is also an activity. There is no way of renouncing work altogether.

The man who works for others, without any selfish motive, really does good to himself.

Perform your duties in an unselfish spirit. Always try to perform your duties without desiring any result.

Ramkrishna

....Do your work, but surrender the result to God.

The love of God grows in the heart through selfless work. Then, through His grace, one realizes Him in course of time and God can be seen. One can talk to Him as I am talking to you.

On Sin

Let him say to God, 'O Lord, I will not repeat such an action', and he need not be afraid of anything.

People who have not realized God get engaged in more and more sinful actions.

One must have this kind of faith: 'Once I have uttered the name of Rama, can I be a sinner any more'?

Sin would have increased if God had not made the sinner feel that he is responsible.

Ramkrishna

All the sins of the body fly away if one chants the name of God and sings his glories.

If a man has faith in God, then even if he has committed the most heinous sins — such as killing a cow, a brahmin, or a woman — he will certainly be saved through his faith.

If you say, 'I am a sinner', eternally, you will remain a sinner to all eternity. You ought rather to repeat, 'I am not bound, I am not bound. Who can bind me? I am the Son of God, the king of kings.

Ramkrishna

Suicide is a heinous sin, undoubtedly. A man who kills himself must return again and again to this world and suffer its agony.

If a man slips from the path of yoga, then he is born in a prosperous family and starts again his spiritual practice for the realisation of God.

On Ma Kali

Ramkrishna

Bondage and liberation are both of Her making. By her maya worldly people get entangled in 'woman' and 'gold', and again through Her grace they attain liberation.

After the destruction of the universe, at the end of a great cycle, the Divine Mother garners the seeds for the next creation.

O Mother, I am the machine and Thou art the operator; I am the chariot and Thou art the driver. I move as Thou movest me; I do as Thou makest me do.

Ramkrishna

It is She who creates and preserves the world, who always protects Her children and who grants whatever they desire: dharma, artha, kama, moksha.

The aim of human life is to attain bhakti. As for other things, the Mother knows best.

On Householders

Ramkrishna

Do your duty with one hand and the other hold to God. After the duty is over, you will hold to God with both hands.

A devotee who can call on God while living a householder's life is a hero indeed.

House, wife and children are all transitory; they only have a momentary existence. The palm-tree alone is real. One or two fruits have dropped off. Why lament?

Ramkrishna

Do all your duties, but keep your mind on God... Treat them (your family) as if they were very dear to you, but know in your heart of hearts that they do not belong to you.

On Company

Ramkrishna

Live in the world like an ant. The world contains a mixture of truth and untruth, sugar and sand. Be an ant and take the sugar.

A man living in society should make a show of tamas to protect himself from evil-minded people. But he should not harm anybody in anticipation of harm likely to be done to him.

Ramkrishna

In God's creation there are all sorts of things. He has created bad men as well as good men. It is He who gives us good tendencies, and it is He again who gives us evil tendencies.

On Teachers & Scriptures

Ramkrishna

To teach others one must have a badge of authority; otherwise teaching becomes a mockery.

Brother, what shall I do with a mere bread-winning education? I would rather acquire that wisdom that would illuminate my heart and give me satisfaction forever.

A preacher may not be a scholarly person, but don't conclude that he lacks wisdom. The wisdom comes from God; it is inexhaustible.

If you have no Guru, then pray to God with a longing heart. He will let you know what He is like.

Ramkrishna

The guru is like a companion who leads you by the hand.

The preacher with a commission from God need not invite people to hear him. He possesses such irresistible attraction that people come to him of their own accord.

God cannot be realised through scholarship. He is beyond the scriptures, the Vedas, Puranas and Tantras.

One can get human gurus by the million. All want to be teachers. But who cares to be a disciple?

Ramkrishna

Nobody can confound a preacher who teaches people after having received the command of God.

Getting a ray of light from the goddess of learning, a man becomes so powerful that before him big scholars seem mere earthworms.

On Ignorance & Knowledge

Ramkrishna

As long as a man remains ignorant, that is to say, as long as he has not realised God, so long will he be born.

....After attaining Knowledge he will not have to come back to this earth or go any other plane of existence.

Futile is the human birth without the awakening of spiritual consciousness.

I and mine indicate ignorance. Without ignorance one cannot have such a feeling as "I am the doer; these are my wife, children and possessions."

Ramkrishna

Everyone can attain Knowledge. There are two entities: jivatma, the individual soul, and Paramatma, the Supreme Soul. Through prayer all individual souls can be united to the Supreme Soul.